BTEC FIRST
Application of Science
Study & Exam Practice

This book is for anyone doing **BTEC Level 2
First Award in Application of Science**.
It covers the examined unit of the course — **Unit 8**.

All the **important topics** are explained in a clear, straightforward
way to help you get all the marks you can in the exam.

It's full of **useful practice questions** to help you get to grips with
the essential science you'll need for the exams.

What CGP is all about

Our sole aim here at CGP is to produce the highest
quality books — carefully written, immaculately presented
and dangerously close to being funny.

Then we work our socks off to get them
out to you — at the cheapest possible prices.

Published by CGP

Editors:
Charlotte Burrows, Jane Sawers, Katherine Craig, Karen Wells, Rachael Rogers.

ISBN: 978 1 84762 869 5

With thanks to Rosie McCurrie for the proofreading.

With thanks to Tom Davies, Rebecca Harvey, John Myers and Gary Talbot for the reviewing.

Printed by Elanders Ltd, Newcastle upon Tyne.
Clipart from Corel®

Based on the classic CGP style created by Richard Parsons.

Contents

Exam Tips

This book is for anyone studying BTEC First Award in Application of Science.

Here is What Will Happen...

There are four units in this course.

Unit 5	
Unit 6	Units 5, 6 and 7 will be assessed by your teacher. Your teacher will set you assignments.
Unit 7	
Unit 8	For Unit 8, you'll have to do an exam.

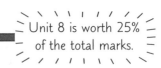

Unit 8 is worth 25% of the total marks.

How to Use This Book

This book is to help you with the Unit 8 exam.

1) The revision pages have all the facts you need to learn.
   - Read a page.
   - Cover it up.
   - Scribble down what you remember.
   - Do this until you can write down all the key points on the page.

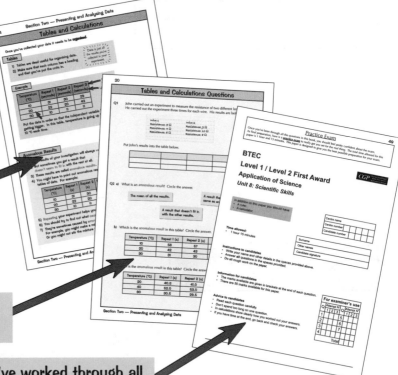

2) Now use the question pages to test you really know your stuff.

3) When you've worked through all the pages do the practice exam paper at the end of the book.

Top Exam Tips

1) Make sure you read all the information given to you in the question.
2) Look at the number of marks on offer to give you an idea of how much to write.
3) If you are asked to calculate something, make sure you show your working.
4) Make sure you understand what the question is asking you to do.
   Take a look at the guide on the next two pages for some handy tips.

Exam Tips

Types of Exam Question

Certain words in an exam question tell you what to do. It's a good idea to learn what these words mean. Then they won't be able to trip you up.

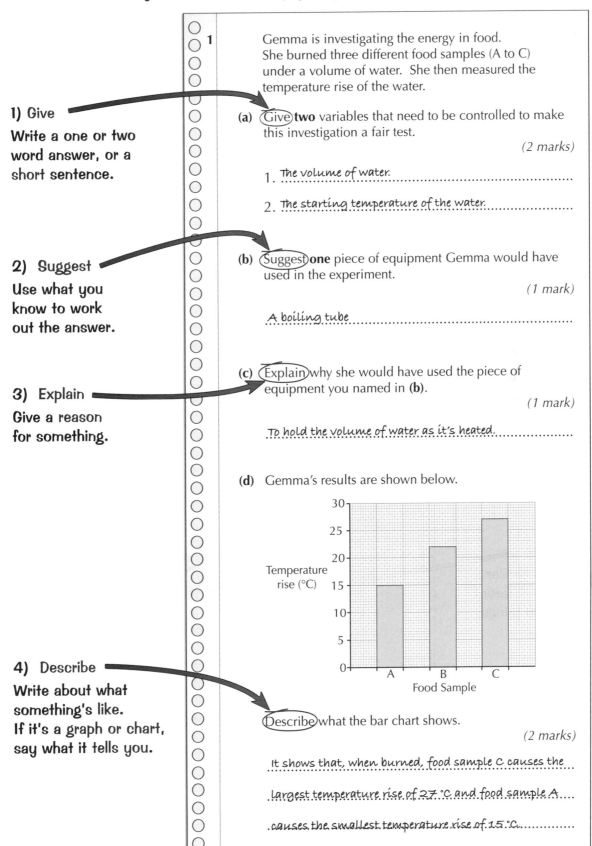

1) Give

Write a one or two word answer, or a short sentence.

2) Suggest

Use what you know to work out the answer.

3) Explain

Give a reason for something.

4) Describe

Write about what something's like. If it's a graph or chart, say what it tells you.

1   Gemma is investigating the energy in food. She burned three different food samples (A to C) under a volume of water. She then measured the temperature rise of the water.

(a) Give two variables that need to be controlled to make this investigation a fair test.

(2 marks)

1. The volume of water.

2. The starting temperature of the water.

(b) Suggest one piece of equipment Gemma would have used in the experiment.

(1 mark)

A boiling tube

(c) Explain why she would have used the piece of equipment you named in (b).

(1 mark)

To hold the volume of water as it's heated.

(d) Gemma's results are shown below.

Temperature rise (°C) — bar chart showing Food Sample A = 15, B = 22, C = 27

Describe what the bar chart shows.

(2 marks)

It shows that, when burned, food sample C causes the largest temperature rise of 27 °C and food sample A causes the smallest temperature rise of 15 °C.

Exam Tips

2 Gary was investigating the current through a resistor. He measured the current at different voltages. Here is a graph of Gary's results.

5) Calculate

Do some maths. Show your working and give your answer with the right units.

(a) Calculate the difference in current between 3 V and 5 V.

(2 marks)

50 A – 30 A = 20 A

(b) Gary repeated his experiment with a different resistor. His results are shown below.

6) Compare

Say what is similar and what is different between two things.

Compare the results for the two resistors.

(3 marks)

For each resistor, as the voltage increases the current increases. For both resistors, as the voltage doubles, the current through the resistor doubles. The current for a certain voltage is always higher through resistor A than resistor B.

Planning Investigations

If you're trying to find something out you need to do an investigation.

Hypothesis

1) The first step in an investigation is to write a hypothesis.
2) A hypothesis says how two or more things could be linked.
3) The hypothesis is tested in an investigation.

Example 1

1) A student is looking at why people have spots.

2) She notices that everyone with spots picks their nose. There seems to be a link between nose picking and spots.

Nose picking = spots?

3) The student thinks that the spots might be caused by people picking their nose. To find out if this is true she needs a hypothesis to test.

4) There are two types of hypothesis she could have:

1) She could just say how something will change in the investigation. For example:

"People who pick their nose more often will get more spots."

2) She could say how the amount of something will change in the investigation. For example:

"People who pick their nose twice as often will have twice as many spots."

Example 2

1) A student is looking at why some plants grow taller than others.

2) He notices that plants in the sun grow taller than those in the shade. There seems to be a link between sunlight and plant growth.

Sunlight = plant growth?

3) The student thinks that plant growth might be caused by sunlight.

4) To find out if this is true he thinks up a hypothesis. For example:

"The greater the amount of sunlight plants get, the taller they will grow."
"Plants that get twice as much sunlight will grow twice as tall."

Planning Investigations

Plan

1) To test a hypothesis you need to have a good plan.
2) A plan says what you're going to do in an investigation and how you're going to do it.
3) Your plan needs to include these things:
   - a method (see below),
   - what equipment you'll use and why (see next page),
   - a risk assessment (see next page),
   - what you'll change during the investigation and what you'll keep the same (see page 10),
   - what you'll measure and how many readings you'll take (see page 11).

Method

A method is a step-by-step list of everything you would do in an experiment.

Example

1) A student is investigating the energy content of food.
2) Her hypothesis is "The more fat in food, the higher the energy content."
3) Here is her method:

Investigation into the Energy Content of Food — Method

1. Weigh the sample of food.
2. Measure out 50 ml of water into a copper calorimeter.
3. Record the temperature of the water.
4. Light the food sample and put it under the calorimeter. Let the food burn out.
5. Make a note of the highest temperature the water reaches.
6. Reweigh any food left.
7. Repeat for samples of food with different amounts of fat.

Someone should be able to repeat the investigation using your method and get similar results. This means it needs to be really clear.
For example, say exactly how much of a chemical you'd use.

A copper calorimeter is just a copper container with a lid.

You also have to make sure that your method will test your hypothesis. For example, here the energy content of the food (temperature change in water) and fat content are measured.

The steps in the method should be in the order you'd carry them out.

Copper calorimeter

Thermometer

Food sample

Planning Investigations

Equipment

1) In your plan you need to list all the equipment you're going to use.

2) You also need to say why you're using each piece of equipment.

3) For example, if you need to measure out some water you would use a measuring cylinder. This is because it is used to measure out volumes of liquid.

4) Using the right equipment will give you accurate results (results near to the real value).

5) For example:

If you need to measure out 11 ml, this measuring cylinder would be great. It's the right size and you can see where 11 ml is.

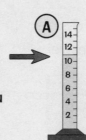

This measuring cylinder isn't as good. It's too big and you can't really see where 11 ml is.

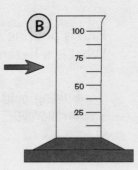

Risk Assessment

1) Part of planning an investigation is doing a risk assessment.

2) A risk assessment helps to make sure the investigation will be safe.

3) You should always make sure that you think of all the hazards (dangers) that you might come across.

4) Hazards are things like...

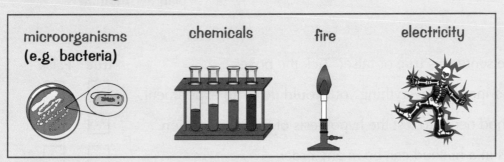

microorganisms (e.g. bacteria)   chemicals   fire   electricity

5) You need to come up with ways of reducing the risks from the hazards you've spotted. For example:

- If you're using acid, wear goggles.
  This will reduce the risk of getting acid in your eyes.
- If you're working with bacteria, wash your hands afterwards.
  This will reduce the risk of taking in bacteria.

6) You need to write about your risk assessment in your plan.

Planning Investigations Questions

Q1 Which of these sentences is **not** a hypothesis? Tick the box.

a) Increasing the temperature will make the reaction go faster. ☐

b) The number of bacteria increases. ☐

c) Doubling the surface area of a parachute will halve the time it takes to fall to the ground. ☐

Q2 Paul is pouring acid into a beaker.
What is a hazard of doing this? Circle the answer.

Spilling acid on his skin.

Getting an electric shock.

Getting bacteria on his skin.

Q3 Fill in the gaps in the sentences. Use the right word from below the gap.

a) To do a risk assessment you need to spot ....
   hazards   mistakes

b) You then need to find ways to .... the risks.
   increase   reduce

c) You need to write about your risk assessment in your ....
   plan   method

Q4 Are these sentences **true** or **false**? Tick the boxes.

	True	False
a) A method includes everything you would do in an experiment.	☐	☐
b) The method needs to test the hypothesis of the investigation.	☐	☐
c) The steps in a method can be in any order.	☐	☐

Q5 You need to measure out **7 ml** of acid.
Circle the piece of equipment you would use. Give a reason for your choice.

Reason: ....

....

....

Planning Investigations Questions

Q6 When magnesium is added to hydrochloric acid, heat is given off. Rana wants to find out how the amount of magnesium affects the amount of heat given off.

> *A hypothesis says how two or more things could be linked.*

a) Complete the **hypothesis** for Rana's investigation below.

Increasing the amount of magnesium used will ....

....

b) Below is a list of **equipment** Rana will use in her investigation.

1) Beaker	4) Thermometer	7) Stopwatch
2) Tongs	5) Dilute hydrochloric acid	8) Safety goggles
3) Measuring cylinder	6) 1 cm strips of magnesium ribbon	9) Lab coat

Why does she need a thermometer?

....

c) Rana has written a **method** for her experiment.
Number the steps 1-4 to put them in the **right order**.
The first one has been done for you.

☐ Add the magnesium ribbon to the beaker and start the stopwatch.

1 Measure out 50 cm³ of hydrochloric acid into a measuring cylinder.

☐ Measure the temperature of the reaction after one minute.

☐ Pour the hydrochloric acid into a beaker.

d) Rana needs to do a **risk assessment** for the investigation.
Write down a **hazard** of her method in **c)**. Then say how she could **reduce this risk**.

> *Think about the equipment she needs for the investigation.*

Hazard: ....

....

To reduce the risk: ....

....

Making a Fair Test

You need to make sure your investigation is a fair test.

Variables

1) In your investigation you must...

> **Only change one thing. Everything else must be kept the same.**

2) The thing that you change is called the **independent variable**.
3) The things that you keep the same are called **control variables**.
   You need to say how you'll keep these things the same.
4) The thing that's measured is called the **dependent variable**.

Example 1

Investigation to see how changing the amount of **light** changes how **tall a plant grows**.

1) Change the amount of **light** the plant gets (the **independent variable**).

2) Keep everything else the same (the **control variables**).

Different amounts of light

Same temperature.   Same type of plant.   Same amount of water.

3) The **dependent variable** is how tall the plant grows — that's what you're **measuring**.

Example 2

Investigation to see how changing the amount of **magnesium** added to acid affects the **reaction temperature**.

1) Change the amount of **magnesium** added to the acid (the **independent variable**).

2) Keep everything else the same (the **control variables**).

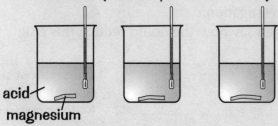

acid
magnesium
Different amounts of magnesium

Same volume of acid.   Same concentration of acid.

3) The **dependent variable** is the **temperature** — that's what you're **measuring**.

Making a Fair Test

Range of Measurements

1) You need to decide what your highest and lowest measurements will be.
   How far apart these are is called the range.
2) You must choose a sensible range. The measurements should not be too close together.
3) Make sure you take enough measurements throughout the range too.
   Three or more measurements should be enough.

Example

Nick wants to know how long a reaction takes at different temperatures.
This means he needs to decide what range of temperatures to use.

| 20 °C   21 °C   22 °C   23 °C |

| 10 °C   20 °C   30 °C   40 °C |

Range = 3 °C. This is a bad range
— the measurements are too close together.

Range = 30 °C. This is a good range
— the measurements are spaced out well.

Repeating Measurements

1) You need to repeat your experiment.
2) The more times you repeat it the better — but three times is usually enough.
3) Then you can work out the mean (average) — see page 15.

Example

1) You want to know how long a reaction takes at 10 °C, 20 °C and 30 °C.
2) Do the reaction three times at each temperature.
3) Time how long it takes each time you do the reaction.

Reaction time at 10 °C

Reaction time at 20 °C

Reaction time at 30 °C

4) You can then put all the results into a table and work out the mean.
   (See pages 14 and 15 for how to do this.)

Making a Fair Test Questions

Q1   Sarah is investigating how changing the **angle of a slope** affects **how far a marble travels**.

angle of slope

distance

a)   What is the **independent** variable? Tick the box.

| The size of the marble. ☐ | The angle of the slope. ☐ | The distance the marble travels. ☐ |

b)   What is the **dependent** variable? Circle the answer.

The angle of the slope.   The distance the marble travels.   The size of the marble.

c)   Which variable needs to be **controlled** in this experiment? Tick the box.

The distance the marble travels.   ☐

The size of the marble.   ☐

The angle of the slope.   ☐

Q2   Mark is investigating how changing the **concentration of Antibiotic X** affects the growth of bacteria. What concentrations of Antibiotic X should he use? Tick the box.

Four measurements
Range: 1.001 mg - 1.004 mg
☐

Two measurements
Range: 1 mg - 500 mg
☐

Four measurements
Range: 1 mg - 15 mg
☐

Q3   Jo is investigating the effect of temperature on the rate of a reaction.
How many **repeats** of the experiment should she do? Circle the answer.

none   one   three

Section One — Planning

Making a Fair Test Questions

Q4   Duncan is investigating the reaction of zinc with hydrochloric acid.
He is finding out how changing the mass of zinc affects the temperature of the reaction.

a)   He knows the reaction works using 2 g of zinc.
Suggest what **measurements** he should use for his experiment.

Choose three or more measurements. They shouldn't be too close together.

....

b)   In the experiment the **volume of acid** needs to be **controlled**.
How could he do this? Tick the box.

By not measuring the volume of acid used. ☐

By using 25 cm³ of acid first, then 50 cm³ of acid after. ☐

By always using 25 cm³ of acid. ☐

acid — zinc

Q5   Ravi and Megan are carrying out an investigation.

> Investigation into the Reaction of Hydrochloric Acid
> with Sodium Hydroxide
>
> Hypothesis:
> Increasing the concentration of acid will increase the
> temperature of the reaction.

a)   What is the **independent** variable in their investigation?

....

....

The independent variable is the variable you change.

b)   What is the **dependent** variable in their investigation?

....

....

The dependent variable is the variable you measure.

c)   The temperature of the acid needs to be controlled.
Give **one other** variable that needs to be controlled.

....

Tables and Calculations

Once you've collected your data it needs to be **organised**.

Tables

1) Tables are dead useful for organising data.
2) Make sure that each column has a heading and that you've put the units in.

Data is just all the results you've collected in your experiment.

Example

Temperature (°C)	Repeat 1 (seconds)	Repeat 2 (seconds)	Repeat 3 (seconds)
10	31	30	29
20	22	20	42
30	10	11	11

Column headings

Units

Put the data in order so that the independent variable is getting bigger. In this table, temperature is going up by 10 °C each time.

Reminder
The independent variable is the thing that you change. Here it is temperature.

Anomalous Results

1) The results of your investigation will always vary a bit.
2) But sometimes you get a result that doesn't seem to fit in with the rest at all.
3) These results are called anomalous results.
4) You might have to point out anomalous results in tables of data. For example:

Results

Anomalous Result

Temperature (°C)	Repeat 1 (s)	Repeat 2 (s)	Repeat 3 (s)
10	31	30	29
20	22	20	42
30	10	11	11

Anomalous result

5) Repeating your experiment helps you to spot anomalous results.
6) You should try to find out what caused them.
7) They're sometimes caused by errors during the experiment.
   For example, you might make a mistake when you're reading a thermometer.
   Or you might not stir the mixture properly during a chemical reaction.

Tables and Calculations

The Mean

1) If you've repeated an investigation you need to work out the mean (average).

2) Just add together the results. Then divide by the total number of results.

3) Don't include any anomalous results when you're working out the mean.

Temperature (°C)	Repeat 1 (s)	Repeat 2 (s)	Repeat 3 (s)	Mean (s)
10	31	30	29	$\frac{(31 + 30 + 29)}{3} = 30$
20	22	20	42	$\frac{(22 + 20)}{2} = 21$
30	10	11	11	$\frac{(10 + 11 + 11)}{3} = 10.7$

Add together the results

Divide by 3 (because there are three results for 10 °C)

Don't include 42 here because it's an anomalous result.

Percentage Change

From a table of data, you can calculate how much something has changed as a percentage.

Example

The table shows how much gas is produced during a reaction at certain times.

Time (s)	0	10	20	30	40	50
Amount of gas (cm^3)	0	34	46	53	60	64

Work out the percentage change in the amount of gas produced between 10 s and 30 s.

1) Find the amount of gas at 10 s (34 cm^3) and 30 s (53 cm^3) from the table.

2) Work out the difference in gas between these two times:
   Difference = amount of gas at 30 s – amount of gas at 10 s = 53 cm^3 – 34 cm^3
   = 19 cm^3

3) Then use this equation:

$$\text{percentage change} = \frac{\text{difference}}{\text{starting amount}} \times 100 = \frac{19}{34} \times 100 = 55.9\%$$

This is the amount of gas at 10 s.

Section Two — Presenting and Analysing Data

Tables and Calculations

Significant Figures

In the exam, you might need to round your answer to a certain number of significant figures.

①	The 1st significant figure (s.f.) is the first digit in a number which isn't a zero. ➡️

For example: **2.03070**

1st s.f.

②	The 2nd, 3rd, 4th, etc. significant figures are digits that come straight after the 1st significant figure. (It doesn't matter whether they are zeros or not). ➡️

For example: **2.03070**

1st 2nd 3rd 4th

③	If you're rounding a number to 3 significant figures then the last digit you write is the 3rd significant figure. ➡️

For example: **2.03**

④	When you're rounding, look at the next digit to the right. If it's 5 or more, round up the last digit. If it's 4 or less, leave the last digit as it is. For example:

Write 54.7631 to 4 significant figures

Look at the 5th significant figure. It's smaller than 5, so leave the 6 as it is.

= 54.76

Write 54.7631 to 3 significant figures

Look at the 4th significant figure. It's bigger than 5, so round the 7 up.

= 54.8

⑤	Using **more** significant figures means you're giving the result **more accurately**.

⑥	Accurate results are those that are **really close** to the true answer.

Section Two — Presenting and Analysing Data

Tables and Calculations

If you can use one equation, you can use them all.

1) Equations can look tricky. They often use symbols to stand for different things.

2) But most of the time, all you have to do is times or divide one number by another.

3) You'll be given any equations you need in the exam question. Hooray.

Example

This table shows the results of a bike race.

	Speed (m/s)	Time (s)
Bob	5	60
Eric	6	75

Work out the distance Bob cycled.

$$\text{distance (m)} = \text{speed (m/s)} \times \text{time (s)}$$

1 Plug in the numbers
(Sometimes you'll need to get them in the right units first — see next page.)

→ distance = speed × time
distance = 5 m/s × 60 s

2 Work out the answer with a calculator.

 → distance = 5 m/s × 60 s
distance = 300

Reminder
You're allowed a calculator in the exam. Make sure you know how to use it.

3 Don't forget the units.

The units of distance are m. → distance = 300 m

Tables and Calculations

Units

1) Before you put numbers into an equation, check that the numbers are in the right units.

2) You'll be told what the right units are for the things in the equation.

Example 1

This table shows the results of a bike race.
Work out the distance Tim cycled.

distance (m) = speed (m/s) × time (s)

	Speed (m/s)	Time (minutes)
Vijay	5	3
Tim	7	2

1 The speed is 7 m/s. The time is 2 minutes.
But to use the equation the time needs to be in seconds.

2 There are 60 seconds in 1 minute.
In 2 minutes, there are 2 × 60 = 120 seconds.

3 Now you can plug the numbers into the equation: distance = speed × time
= 7 m/s × 120 s
= 840 m

Example 2

This table shows the force used to move two toy cars.
Work out the work done by Car A.

work done (J) = force (N) × distance (m)

	Force (N)	Distance (cm)
Car A	5	157
Car B	10	223

1 The force is 5 N. The distance the car travelled is 157 cm.
To use the equation the distance needs to be in metres.

2 There are 100 centimetres in 1 metre.
157 cm is 157 ÷ 100 = 1.57 m.

3 Now you can plug the numbers into the equation: work done (J) = force (N) × distance (m)
= 5 N × 1.57 m
= 7.85 J

Section Two — Presenting and Analysing Data

Tables and Calculations

Formula Triangles

A formula triangle can help you rearrange an equation.
Here's how to make a formula triangle...

If 2 letters are multiplied together in the equation, they go on the bottom of the triangle. (The other letter goes on top.)

distance = speed × time

can be written as:

d = s × t

It will then fit into a formula triangle.

If one thing's divided by another in the equation then the one on top of the division goes on top in the triangle. (Then it doesn't matter which way round the other two go on the bottom.)

$$\text{resistance} = \frac{\text{voltage}}{\text{current}}$$

can be written as: $R = \dfrac{V}{I}$

It will then fit into a formula triangle.

Using a Formula Triangle

1) Write down the thing you want, and put '=' after it.
2) In the triangle, cover up the thing you want to find, and write down what's left showing.
3) You've now got the equation — stick the numbers in and you're done.

Example

t = ? ➡ ➡  ➡ This means $t = \dfrac{d}{s}$

Tables and Calculations Questions

Q1   John carried out an experiment to measure the resistance of two different lengths of wire.
He carried out the experiment three times for each wire. His results are below.

> Wire 1
> Resistance: 5 Ω
> Resistance: 4 Ω
> Resistance: 5 Ω
>
> Wire 2
> Resistance: 9 Ω
> Resistance: 10 Ω
> Resistance: 8 Ω

Put John's results into the table below.

Q2 a)   What is an **anomalous result**? Circle the answer.

The mean of all the results.

A result that is the same as another result.

A result that doesn't fit in with the other results.

b)   Which is the **anomalous result** in this table? Circle the answer.

Temperature (°C)	Repeat 1 (s)	Repeat 2 (s)	Repeat 3 (s)
10	56	57	55
20	42	43	42
30	31	30	43

c)   Which is the **anomalous result** in this table? Circle the answer.

Temperature (°C)	Repeat 1 (s)	Repeat 2 (s)	Repeat 3 (s)
20	40.5	41.0	49.5
40	52.0	53.0	51.5
60	30.5	29.5	31.0

Tables and Calculations Questions

Q3 How do you calculate the **mean** of these results? Tick the box.

Drink	Mass of sugar (g)			Mean
	Repeat 1	Repeat 2	Repeat 3	
1	13	10	12	

☐ $(13 + 10 + 12) \times 3$ ☐ $\dfrac{13 + 10 + 12}{3}$ ☐ $13 + 10 + 12$

Q4 Nadia does an experiment to test the effect of two antibiotics.
She repeats the experiment three times. Calculate the **means** of the results below.

Antibiotic	Space around antibiotic disc (mm)			Mean
	Repeat 1	Repeat 2	Repeat 3	
A	7	6	8	....
B	1	3	2	....

Q5 Calculate the **means** for the results below. Give the answers to **3 significant figures**.

Temperature (°C)	Time (s)			Mean
	Repeat 1	Repeat 2	Repeat 3	
10	52	53	52	....
20	40	40	41	....
30	29	28	31	....

Tables and Calculations Questions

Q6   How would you rearrange this equation to work out **mass**?
Use the formula triangle to help you. Circle the answer.

Equation: **force = mass × acceleration**
F   =   m   × a

Formula triangle:

mass = force × acceleration

$$mass = \frac{acceleration}{force}$$

$$mass = \frac{force}{acceleration}$$

Q7   The table shows the force used to move two blocks covered with sandpaper.

	Force (N)	Distance (m)	Work done (J)
Block 1	5.2	0.25	....
Block 2	12.6	0.5	....

a)   Use this equation to complete the table.   **work done (J) = force (N) × distance (m)**

b)   A third block was moved **1200 cm**. How far is this in **metres**?

100 cm = 1 m

....

Q8   The table shows the mass of product formed in a reaction over time.

Time (s)	0	10	20	30
Mass (g)	0	6	10	13

a)   Work out the **difference** between the mass of the product at 10 and at 20 s.

....

b)   Calculate the **percentage change** in the
mass of product made between 10 and 20 s.
Give your answer to **3 significant figures**.

$$percentage \atop change = \frac{difference}{starting\ amount} \times 100$$

Use your answer to **a)** to help you.

....

....

Tables and Calculations Questions

Q9 Calum carried out an experiment to measure how temperature affects the rate of a reaction. He timed how long it took for the reaction to finish at four different temperatures. He carried out his experiment three times. His results are shown below.

Temperature (°C)	Time (s)			Mean
	Repeat 1	Repeat 2	Repeat 3	
40	71.5	72.0	70.5	71.3
50	58.0	59.0	59.0	58.7
60	43.0	41.5	42.5	
70	22.0	21.5	33.5	

a) There is an anomalous result in Calum's data.
Circle the **anomalous result** in Calum's data.

b) Which is a possible **reason** for Calum's anomalous result? Tick the box.

☐ He didn't repeat the experiment enough times.

☐ He didn't leave the reaction for long enough.

☐ The reaction wasn't at the correct temperature.

c) Calculate the **mean** of Calum's results at **60 °C**.
Give your answer to **3 significant figures**.

Here, you can work out the mean by adding the numbers together and dividing by three.

....

....

....

d) Calculate the **mean** of Calum's results at **70 °C**.
Give your answer to **3 significant figures**.

Don't forget to ignore any anomalous results when working out the mean.

....

....

....

e) At which temperature is the reaction **fastest**?

....

Drawing Graphs

Charts and graphs are really good ways of showing your results.
You can use different graphs and charts depending on what you've been measuring.

Bar Charts

1) Bar charts are great when the thing you're measuring has got categories.
2) Categories are things like blood type or ice cream flavour.
3) You can't get results in-between categories.
4) There are some rules you need to follow for drawing bar charts...

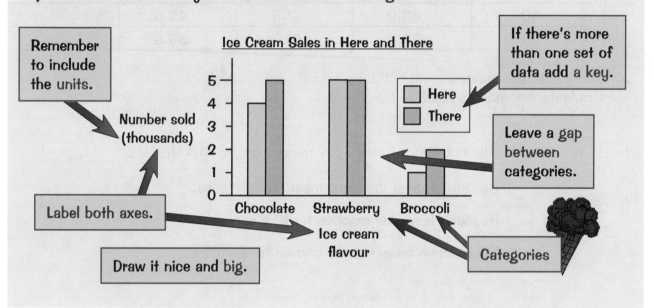

Remember to include the units.

If there's more than one set of data add a key.

Number sold (thousands)

Leave a gap between categories.

Label both axes.

Draw it nice and big.

Categories

Ice Cream Sales in Here and There

Ice cream flavour

Example

Sasha has recorded the mass of carbohydrate, protein and fat in two different foods.

Draw a bar chart to show this data.

Food Group	Food A (g)	Food B (g)
Carbohydrate	18	22
Protein	29	17
Fat	6	12

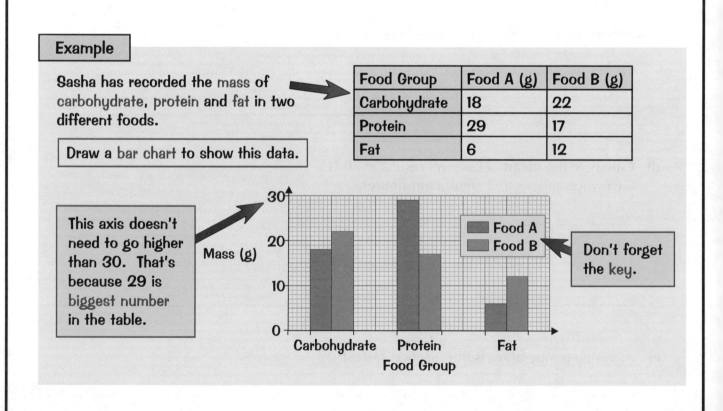

This axis doesn't need to go higher than 30. That's because 29 is biggest number in the table.

Mass (g)

Don't forget the key.

Food Group

Drawing Graphs

Pie Charts

1) Pie charts are also good when the thing you're measuring has got categories.

2) The size of each sector shows the proportion of the total data in that category. For example, half of Jack's class is female and half is male.

male | female

Drawing Pie Charts

The table below shows the results of a survey on the animals people are most afraid of.

Creature	Hamsters	Guinea pigs	Rabbits	Ducks	Stick insects	Total
Number of people	20	17	15	26	12	90

To draw a pie chart of this data, there are some rules you need to follow...

1. Add up all the numbers in each sector to get the total (here it's 90).

2. Then divide 360 by the total. So, $\frac{360}{90} = 4$.

3. Now multiply every result by this number to get the angle for each group. For example, the angle for hamsters is $20 \times 4 = 80°$. The angle for rabbits is $15 \times 4 = 60°$.

4. Draw a 'start line' in a circle and draw the angle of one group from this line. Then carry on to draw the rest of the angles.

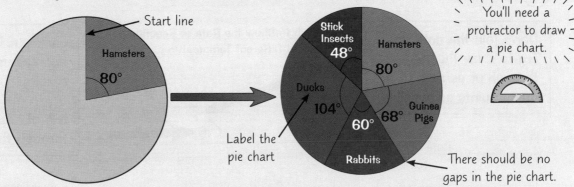

Start line

Hamsters 80°

Stick Insects 48°

Hamsters 80°

Ducks 104°

68° Guinea Pigs

60°

Rabbits

Label the pie chart

You'll need a protractor to draw a pie chart.

There should be no gaps in the pie chart.

5. To check your work, add up all of the angles. You should get 360°. For example, $80° + 68° + 60° + 104° + 48° = 360°$.

Drawing Graphs

Line Graphs

1) If you're measuring something that can have any value you should use a line graph to show the data.

2) For example, temperatures and people's heights would be shown using a line graph.

3) Here are the rules for drawing line graphs...

① First, plot the results on some graph paper, using a cross for each point.

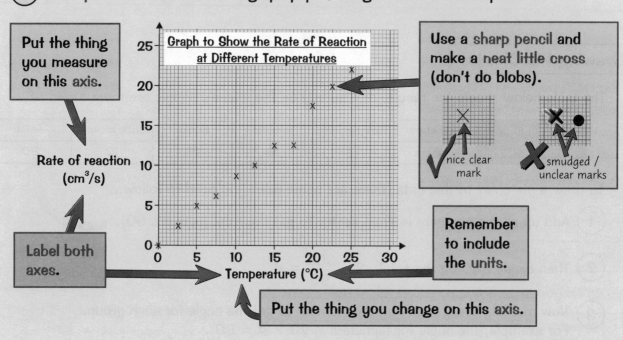

Put the thing you measure on this axis.

Use a sharp pencil and make a neat little cross (don't do blobs).

nice clear mark

smudged / unclear marks

Label both axes.

Remember to include the units.

Put the thing you change on this axis.

② Then draw a line of best fit:

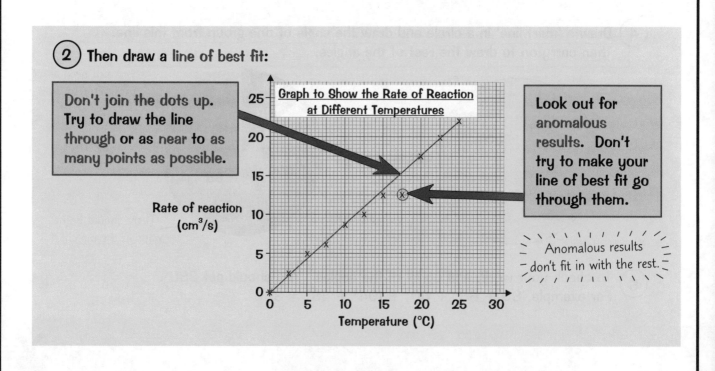

Don't join the dots up. Try to draw the line through or as near to as many points as possible.

Look out for anomalous results. Don't try to make your line of best fit go through them.

Anomalous results don't fit in with the rest.

Drawing Graphs

Curve of Best Fit

1) Sometimes the points you plot on a line graph will form a curve.

2) This means you need to draw a curve of best fit.

3) Here are some rules for drawing a curve of best fit...

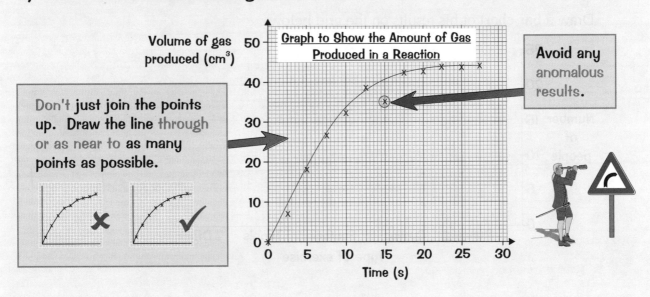

Don't just join the points up. Draw the line through or as near to as many points as possible.

Avoid any anomalous results.

Graph Scales

When you draw a graph, you need to use a sensible scale.

Choose a scale that takes up as much of the graph paper as possible.

Example

Draw a line graph of the data in the table below.

Current (A)	2	3	4	5	6	7	8	9	10
Voltage (V)	1.9	3.2	3.8	5.0	5.8	7.2	7.8	8.4	9.8

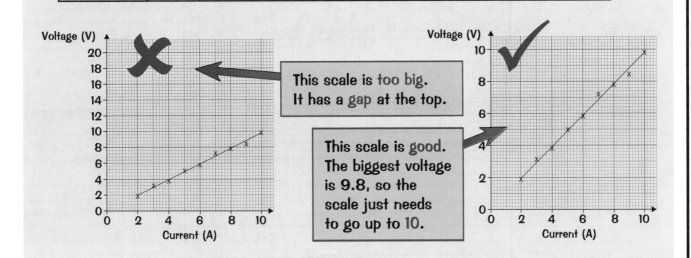

This scale is too big. It has a gap at the top.

This scale is good. The biggest voltage is 9.8, so the scale just needs to go up to 10.

Drawing Graphs Questions

Q1 Yasir did a survey asking people what type of exercise they do most often. His results are in the table below.

Type of exercise	Running	Cycling	Football	Tennis	Other
Number of people	22	15	17	9	11

Draw a **bar chart** of his results on the grid below.

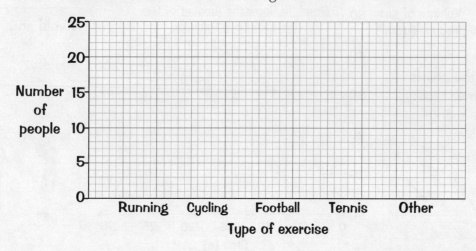

Q2 Chris carried out an experiment to find the energy content of four food samples. Her results are in the table on the right.

Draw a **bar chart** of her results on the grid below.

Food Sample	Energy (J/g)
A	29
B	11
C	37
D	16

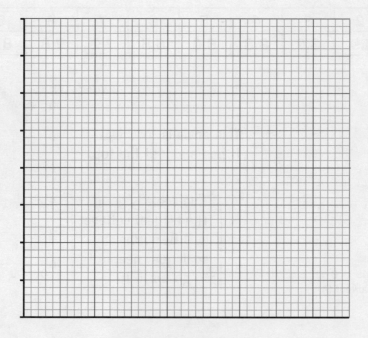

Section Two — Presenting and Analysing Data

Drawing Graphs Questions

Q3 Liz carried out a survey on two year groups to find out students' weights. She then calculated the average weight per person.
Her results are in the table on the right.

Year	Average Weight (kg)	
	Male	Female
10	54	51
11	57	53

Draw a **bar chart** of her results on the grid below.

Don't forget the key.

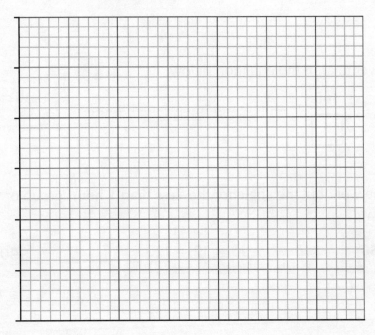

Q4 Josh has recorded the mass of different food groups in one type of food. His results are shown in the table on the right.

Food group	Mass (g)	Angle (°)
carbohydrate	7	84
protein	10	120
fat	5	60
fibre	6	72
other	2	24

Josh wants to draw a pie chart of the results. He has worked out the angle of each sector.
Use the angles in the table to **complete the pie chart** on the right.

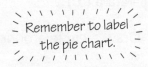
Remember to label the pie chart.

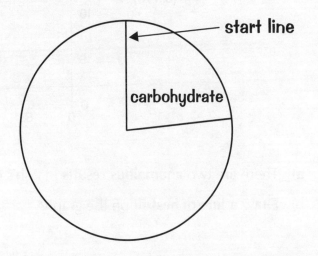
start line
carbohydrate

Section Two — Presenting and Analysing Data

Drawing Graphs Questions

Q5 Richard did a survey to find out how much exercise people do in a week. His results are shown on the right.

Exercise time	Number of people
less than 1 hour	10
1-2 hours	4
3-4 hours	9
5-6 hours	4
more than 6 hours	3

Richard is going to draw a pie chart.

a) Work out the **total** number of people Richard surveyed.

....

b) Use your answer to a) in the equation below.

total number of people → $\dfrac{360}{\boxed{}}$ = ...

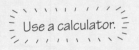

Use a calculator.

c) How should he work out the angle for the '**less than 1 hour**' group of the pie chart? Circle the answer.

$10 \times 5 = 50°$ $10 \times 12 = 120°$ $360 \div 10 = 36°$

Q6 Ash carried out an experiment to investigate how temperature affects the rate of a reaction. He plotted his results on the graph below.

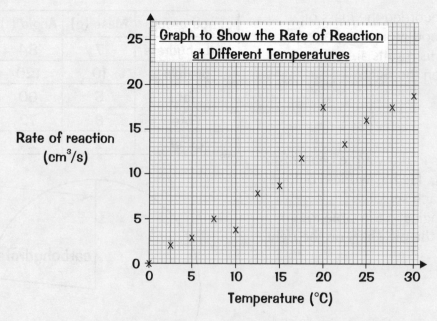

a) There are two **anomalous results** in Ash's data. Draw a circle around each of them.

b) Draw a **line of best fit** on the graph.

Drawing Graphs Questions

Q7 Paul carried out a chemical reaction and recorded how much product was formed over time. His results are shown in the table below.

Time (s)	Mass (g)
0	0
5	4
10	12
15	17
20	19
25	19
30	23
35	24
40	25
45	25
50	25

a) **Plot** Paul's results on the grid below.

Don't forget to label the axes and say what the units are.

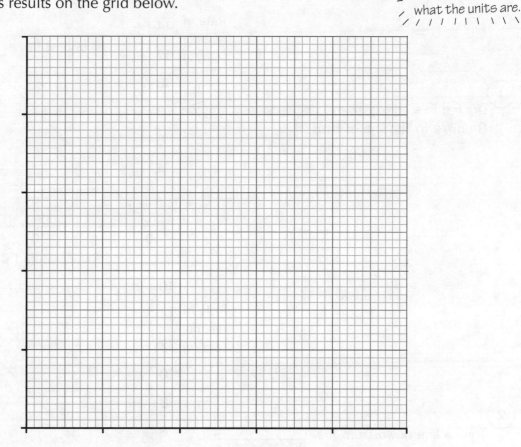

b) Draw a circle around the **anomalous result** on the graph.

c) Draw a **curve of best fit** on the graph.

Data From Graphs

Graphs are really useful because you can find things out from them.

Reading Numbers From Graphs

In the exam you might need to find a value (number) from a graph.

Example 1

The graph on the right shows the
rate of a reaction at different temperatures.

10 °C   15 °C   20 °C

What is the temperature when
the rate of reaction is 8 cm³/s?

① Draw a line across from
8 cm³/s to the line of best fit.

line of best fit

② Draw a line down from the
line of best fit to the x-axis.

③ Read off the value on the
x-axis. It is 10 °C.

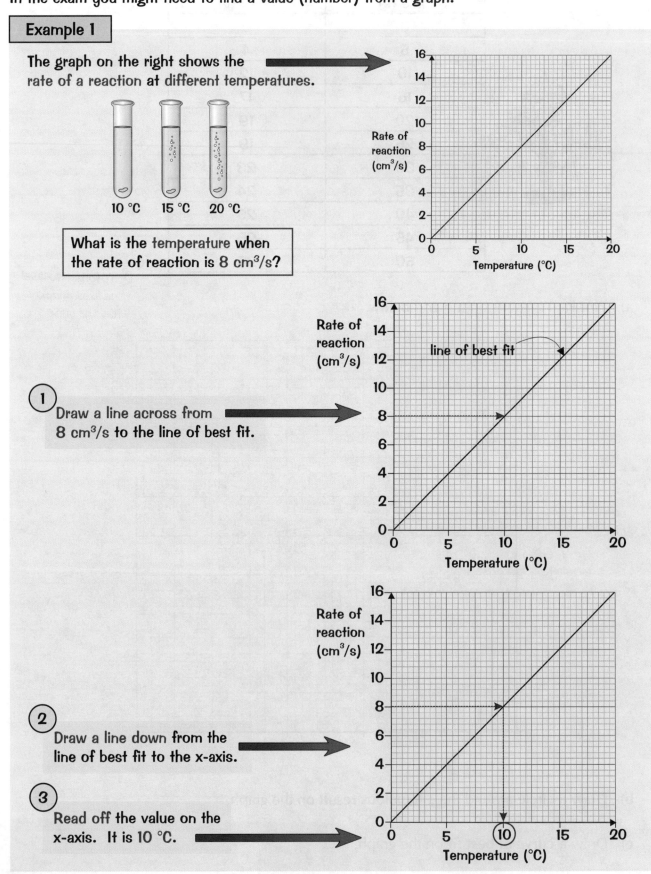

Data From Graphs

Example 2

The graph on the right shows how a person's heart rate changes during a race.

What is the heart rate at 20 seconds?

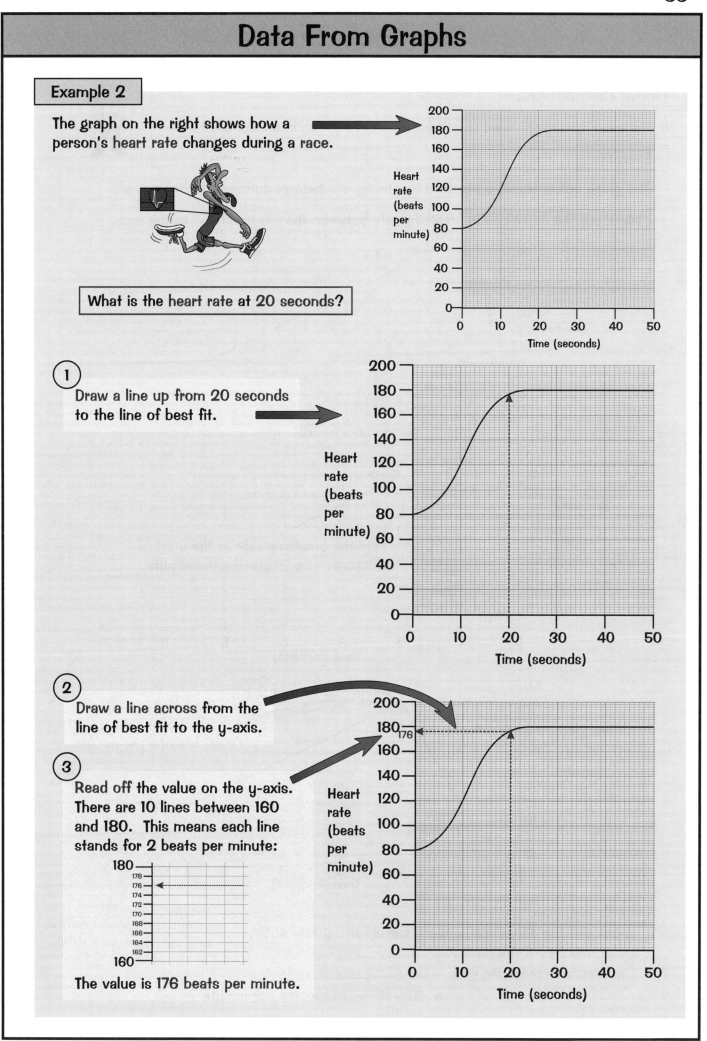

① Draw a line up from 20 seconds to the line of best fit.

② Draw a line across from the line of best fit to the y-axis.

③ Read off the value on the y-axis. There are 10 lines between 160 and 180. This means each line stands for 2 beats per minute:

The value is 176 beats per minute.

Data From Graphs

Doing Calculations

In the exam you might need to use values from a graph in a calculation.

Example

The graph below shows a person's breathing rate before, during and after a race.

> Work out the difference in breathing rate between the start and end of the race.

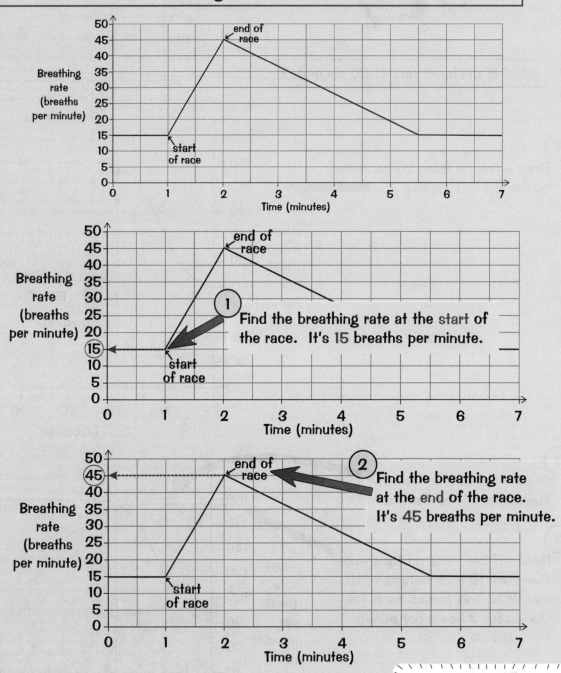

① Find the breathing rate at the start of the race. It's 15 breaths per minute.

② Find the breathing rate at the end of the race. It's 45 breaths per minute.

③ Work out the difference between the breathing rate at the start and end of the race:

Difference in breathing rate = breathing rate at end – breathing rate at start

= 45 – 15 = 30 breaths per minute

> To work out the difference you need to take the smaller number away from the larger number.

Section Two — Presenting and Analysing Data

Data From Graphs

Gradients

In the exam you might need to work out the gradient (slope) of a graph.

y-axis

gradient

x-axis

Example

The graph below is a speed-time graph. It shows the speed of a car over time.

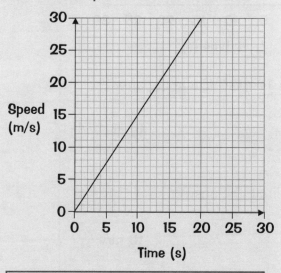

Speed (m/s)

Time (s)

Work out the gradient of the graph.

①

Mark two points anywhere on the line. Use the points to draw a right-angled triangle as shown below.

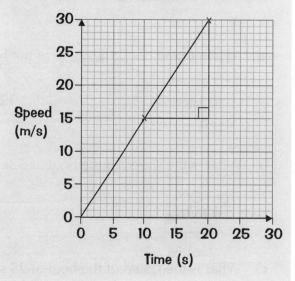

Speed (m/s)

Time (s)

②

Use the lines you have drawn to find the change in y and the change in x.

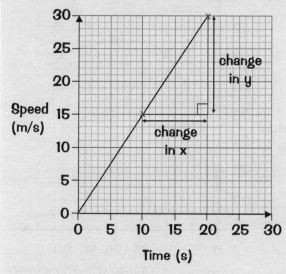

Speed (m/s)

change in y

change in x

Time (s)

Change in y = 30 − 15 = 15 m/s

Change in x = 20 − 10 = 10 s

③

Use this equation to work out the gradient:

$$\text{Gradient} = \frac{\text{change in y}}{\text{change in x}}$$

$$\text{Gradient} = \frac{15}{10} = 1.5$$

1) Sometimes the gradient can tell you something about the data.

2) For example, the gradient of a speed-time graph tells you the acceleration. This means the car in the example has an acceleration of 1.5 m/s².

Acceleration is how fast the car is speeding up.

Data From Graphs Questions

Q1   The graph on the right is a
speed-time graph for a boat.

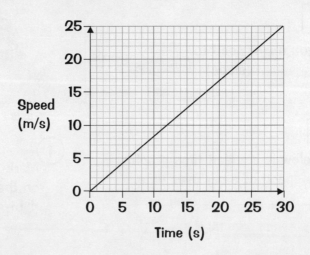

a)   At what time does the speed of the boat reach 10 m/s? Circle the answer.

| 10 seconds | 12 seconds | 15 seconds |

b)   What is the speed of the boat at 5 seconds? Circle the answer.

| 4 m/s | 5 m/s | 10 m/s |

c)   What is the speed of the boat at **25 seconds**?

.... m/s

Q2   The graph on the right shows
how the **temperature** of a
reaction changes over **time**.

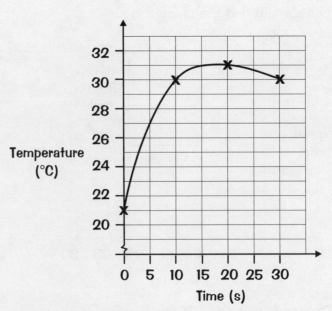

a)   How would you work out the
difference in temperature between
0 seconds and **15 seconds**?
Tick the answer.

30 – 21 = 9 °C   ☐

31 – 21 = 10 °C   ☐

31 – 20 = 11 °C   ☐

b)   What is the difference between the temperature at **5 seconds** and **30 seconds**?

....

Section Two — Presenting and Analysing Data

Data From Graphs Questions

Q3   The graph below shows how Pete's **heart rate** changes during part of a race.

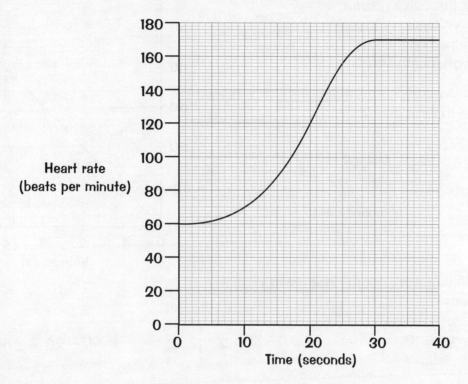

Heart rate
(beats per minute)

Time (seconds)

a)   What is Pete's heart rate at **20 seconds**?
Tick the answer.

140 beats per minute ☐   100 beats per minute ☐

120 beats per minute ☐   126 beats per minute ☐

b)   What is Pete's heart rate at **10 seconds**?
Circle the answer.

| 70 beats per minute | 74 beats per minute | 68 beats per minute |

c)   What is Pete's heart rate at **35 seconds**?

.... beats per minute

d)   At what **time** has Pete's heart rate reached **80 beats per minute**?

.... seconds

38

Data From Graphs Questions

Q4 The graph on the right shows the **current** through a resistor at different **voltages**. A triangle has been drawn on the graph to help you work out the **gradient**.

A resistor is part of an electrical circuit.

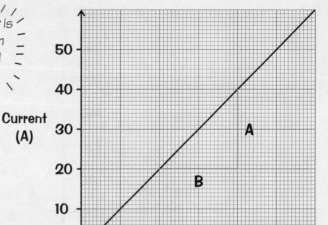

a) Draw lines to match up the **sides** of the **triangle** to what they show.

| A | | change in x |
| B | | change in y |

b) How would you work out the **change in** y? Circle the answer.

    30 – 20 = 10   4 – 2 = 2   40 – 20 = 20

c) Work out the **change in** x.

....

d) Below is a voltage-current graph for a different resistor.

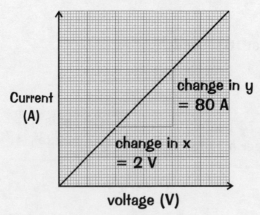

The change in y is **80** A. The change in x is **2** V.
Use this equation to work out the gradient of the graph:

$$\text{Gradient} = \frac{\text{change in y}}{\text{change in x}}$$

....

....

....

Data From Graphs Questions

Q5   Sarah timed **how long** it took to walk to school in seconds.
She also measured the **distance** she walked in metres.
Then she plotted her results on the graph shown below.

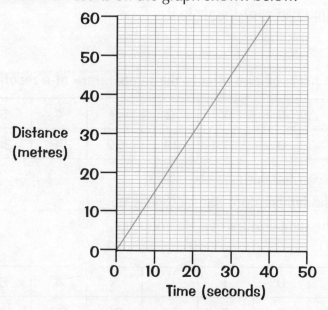

a)   How long did it take Sarah to walk **30 metres**?

....

b)   How far had Sarah walked after **25 seconds**?

....

c)   Work out the **distance** Sarah walked between **25 seconds** and **40 seconds**.
Use your answer to part **b)** to help you.

....

....

d)   Work out the **gradient** of the graph.

change in y = ...

change in x = ...

gradient = ...

$$\text{Gradient} = \frac{\text{change in y}}{\text{change in x}}$$

....

....

Section Two — Presenting and Analysing Data

Interpreting Graphs and Tables

Tables and graphs can show you the trends (patterns) in your results.

Trends in Tables

Once your data is in a table, you can spot trends in it.

Example

Farish is looking at how the mass of zinc affects the temperature of a reaction with acid.

Mass (g)	0	1	2	3	4	5	6
Temperature rise (°C)	0	7	14	22	28	36	44

From his results table, you can tell that:

1) As the mass goes up, the temperature rise also goes up.

2) As the mass doubles, the temperature rise also doubles.

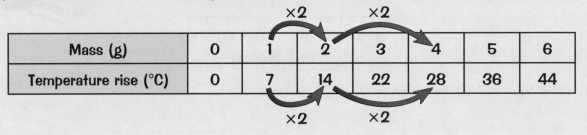

Mass (g)	0	1	2	3	4	5	6
Temperature rise (°C)	0	7	14	22	28	36	44

Correlation in Graphs

1) Line graphs are great for showing the relationship (the link) between two things.

2) The relationship is called a correlation.

Positive Correlation

As one thing increases so does the other.

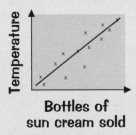

Bottles of sun cream sold

As the temperature increases the amount of sun cream sold also increases.

Negative Correlation

As one thing increases the other decreases.

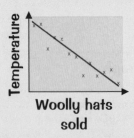

Woolly hats sold

As the temperature increases the number of hats sold decreases.

No Correlation

There's no relationship between the two things.

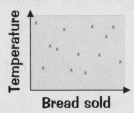

Bread sold

The temperature has no effect on the amount of bread sold.

Interpreting Graphs and Tables

Quantitative Relationships

1) Sometimes both things shown on a line graph change by a certain amount.
2) This is called a quantitative relationship.

Example

The graph below shows speed against time for a moving car.

Describe the trend shown in the graph.

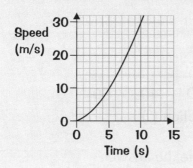

1) On the graph, when time increases from 5 seconds to 10 seconds, speed increases from 10 m/s to 30 m/s.
2) This means that as time doubles the speed of the car triples.

'Triples' means times by three.

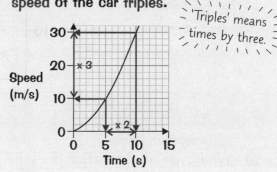

Proportional Graphs

The are two special types of quantitative relationship you need to know about.

Directly Proportional

Both things increase (or decrease) by the same amount.

For example, as one thing doubles (x 2), the other thing also doubles (x 2).

Indirectly Proportional

As one thing increases, the other thing decreases by the same amount.

For example, as one thing doubles (x 2), the other thing halves (÷ 2).

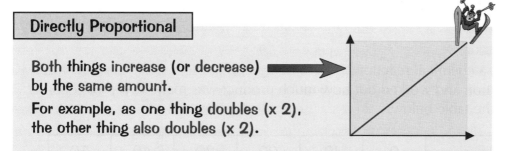

Interpreting Graphs and Tables Questions

Q1 Raja did an experiment to investigate the link between the **angle of incidence** and the **angle of reflection**. She plotted a line graph of her results.

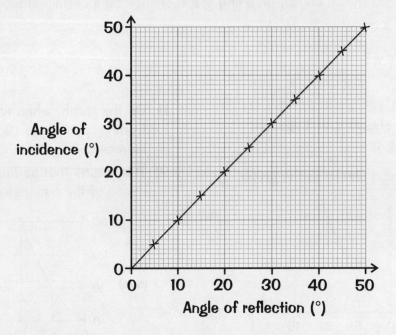

a) What type of **correlation** does the graph show? Circle the answer.

Positive correlation   Negative correlation   No correlation

b) What type of **relationship** does the graph show? Circle the answer.

Directly proportional   Indirectly proportional

Q2 Simon carried out a chemical reaction.
He timed the reaction and worked out how much product was made every 10 seconds.
His results are in the table below.

Time (s)	0	10	20	30	40	50
Mass of product (g)	0	2	4	6	8	10

What **trend** do the results show? Tick the box.

☐ As time increases, the mass of product made decreases.

☐ As time doubles, the mass of product made doubles.

☐ As time doubles, the mass of product made halves.

Interpreting Graphs and Tables Questions

Q3   Lucy was investigating the reaction between hydrochloric acid and sodium hydroxide. She wanted to find out how the **concentration** of hydrochloric acid affects the **temperature rise** of the reaction. Her results are shown in the graph below.

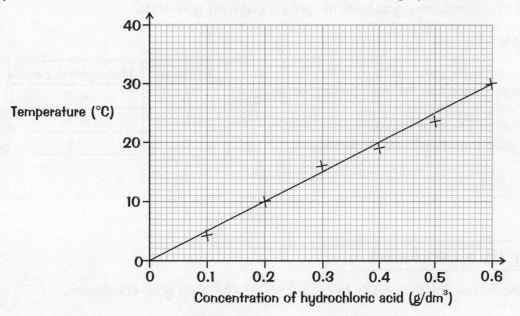

Describe the **trend** shown by the graph by answering these questions.

a)   What sort of **correlation** does the graph show? Tick the box.

☐ Positive correlation.

☐ Negative correlation.

☐ No correlation.

b)   Complete the sentence below by circling the right word.

As the concentration of hydrochloric acid increases, the temperature **increases / decreases**.

c)   The graph shows a **quantitative relationship**. Describe what happens to the variables.

....

....

....

You need to say what happens to the concentration and temperature in terms of numbers.

d)   Is the relationship shown on the graph **directly proportional** or **indirectly proportional**?

....

Conclusion and Evaluation

You have to finish an investigation with a conclusion and an evaluation.

Coming to a Conclusion

To come to a conclusion, you have to analyse (look at) your data.

Example

Pea plants were grown with different fertilisers.
The table shows how tall the plants grew.

Conclusion: Fertiliser B makes pea plants
grow taller than fertiliser A or fertiliser C.

Fertiliser	Mean growth / mm
A	13.5
B	19.5
C	5.5

Backing Up a Conclusion

You should use the data that's been collected to back up your conclusion.

Example

Fertiliser B made the pea plants grow more than fertiliser A.
The mean growth for fertiliser B was 19.5 mm and only 13.5 mm for fertiliser A.

The Hypothesis

1) Look back to the hypothesis. If the conclusion agrees with the hypothesis,
    it makes us more sure that the hypothesis is right.
2) If the conclusion doesn't agree with the hypothesis, it makes us less sure that it's right.
3) You need to be able to say how well the conclusion agrees with the hypothesis.

Example

For the fertiliser experiment, the hypothesis was:

> *"Fertiliser B will be more effective at making plants grow than fertilisers A and C."*

*   The conclusion partly agrees with this hypothesis — fertiliser B is more effective
    than fertilisers A and C at making pea plants grow.
*   However, the conclusion doesn't prove that fertiliser B is more effective than
    fertilisers A and C at making all types of plant grow.

Conclusion and Evaluation

Evaluating the Method

In an evaluation you say how well your investigation went and if there were any problems. In the exam you might have to evaluate someone else's investigation...

1) Think about whether the results were accurate.
   - Were the measurements taken carefully?
   - Were there any problems with the equipment?
   - Was it difficult to measure or time anything?

Reminder
Accurate results are ones near to the real value.

Example

Sam measured out 25 cm³ acid for a reaction. He used a measuring cylinder with a scale divided up into 50 cm³ sections. Sam's results were not what he expected. It might be because he didn't read the scale on the measuring cylinder carefully.

2) Look to see if repeating the experiment gave the same results. If you get the same results, you can be more sure that they're right.

3) Were there any anomalous results? Think about why they might have happened.

Improving the Experiment

1) In the exam, you might be asked how you could change a method to improve it.
2) Look back at the problems you came up with and say how you could fix them.

Example

Sam could use a different measuring cylinder — one that is divided up into smaller units. This would mean he could read the volume more accurately.

Extending the Experiment

1) In the exam, you might have to suggest ways of taking an investigation further.
2) This helps you find more support for the hypothesis.

Example

For the fertiliser investigation, repeat the experiment using a different type of plant. This will show if fertiliser B is still more effective at making plants grow than fertilisers A and C (see the previous page).

Conclusion and Evaluation Questions

Q1 Jason carried out an experiment to find out how much heat energy is made by burning different foods. He tested three different foods. He recorded his results in the table below.

Food sample	Repeat 1 (kJ/g)	Repeat 2 (kJ/g)	Repeat 3 (kJ/g)	Mean (kJ/g)
A	37.0	35.0	36.5	36.2
B	15.0	14.0	16.0	15.0
C	23.5	23.0	23.0	23.2

What **conclusion** can Jason draw from his results? Tick the box.

☐ Food sample A produces more heat energy than any other food sample when burnt.

☐ Food sample A produces more heat energy than samples B or C when burnt.

☐ Food sample C produces the least energy of all the food samples when burnt.

Q2 Sally carried out an experiment to find out the effect of temperature on the rate of a reaction. Her hypothesis was:

The higher the temperature, the higher the rate of the reaction will be.

Her results are shown in the graph below.

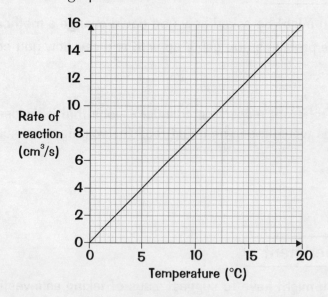

a) What **conclusion** can be drawn from Sally's results? Tick the box.

☐ Temperature doesn't affect the rate of the reaction.

☐ As temperature increases, the rate of reaction decreases.

☐ As temperature increases, the rate of reaction also increases.

b) Do Sally's results **support** her hypothesis? Circle the answer. **yes / no**

Conclusion and Evaluation Questions

Q3 Lisa is investigating how increasing the voltage across a thermistor affects the current flowing through it. Her results are shown in the graph below.

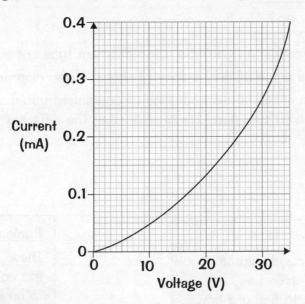

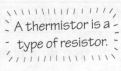
A thermistor is a type of resistor.

a) What **conclusion** can be drawn from the results?

....

....

b) Lisa's hypothesis was:

'As voltage increases, the current through the thermistor will decrease.'

Do her results **support** the hypothesis? Tick the box.

☐ Yes   ☐ No

Give a **reason** for your answer.

Look at your answer to (a) and decide whether it matches the hypothesis.

....

....

c) Lisa thinks that her results aren't very accurate.
Suggest **one** reason why Lisa's results might not be accurate.

....

....

Section Three — Conclusion and Evaluation

Laboratory Equipment

If you do an investigation at school you'll carry it out in a laboratory.
In an investigation you'll use all sorts of equipment...

Different Types of Equipment

1) If you do a chemistry investigation you'll be using different types of equipment.

2) This means you might use some of the equipment shown in the diagram below.

3) In the exam you might be asked about what kind of equipment you'd use in an experiment. This means it's a good idea to remember the different types...

Example

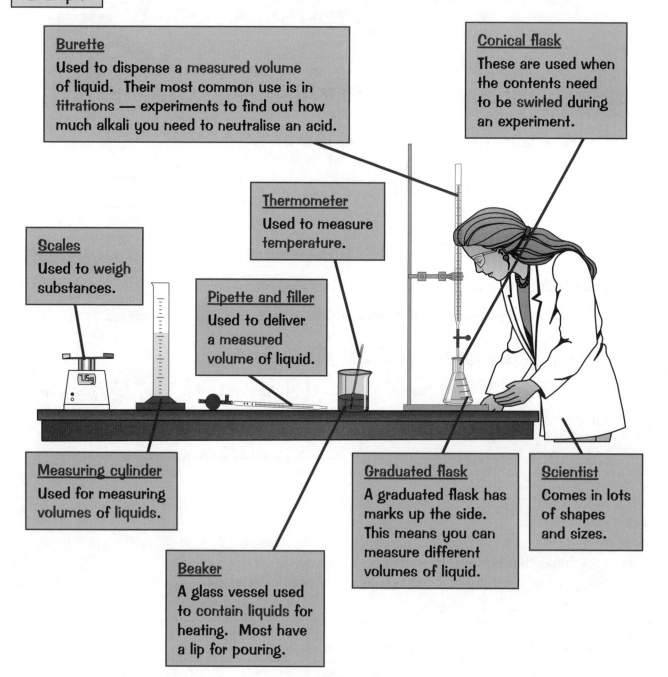

Burette
Used to dispense a measured volume of liquid. Their most common use is in titrations — experiments to find out how much alkali you need to neutralise an acid.

Conical flask
These are used when the contents need to be swirled during an experiment.

Thermometer
Used to measure temperature.

Scales
Used to weigh substances.

Pipette and filler
Used to deliver a measured volume of liquid.

Measuring cylinder
Used for measuring volumes of liquids.

Graduated flask
A graduated flask has marks up the side. This means you can measure different volumes of liquid.

Scientist
Comes in lots of shapes and sizes.

Beaker
A glass vessel used to contain liquids for heating. Most have a lip for pouring.

Practice Exam

Once you've been through all the questions in this book, you should feel pretty confident about the exam.
As final preparation, here is a **practice exam** to really get you set for the real thing. The total time allowed for this paper is 1 hour and 15 minutes. This paper is designed to give you the best possible preparation for your exam.

BTEC

Level 1 / Level 2 First Award

Application of Science

Unit 8: Scientific Skills

In addition to this paper you should have:
- A ruler.
- A calculator.

Centre name				
Centre number				
Candidate number				

Surname	
Other names	
Candidate signature	

Time allowed:
- 1 hour 15 minutes

Instructions to candidates
- Write your name and other details in the spaces provided above.
- Answer **all** questions in the spaces provided.
- Do all rough work on the paper.

Information for candidates
- The marks available are given in brackets at the end of each question.
- There are 50 marks available for this paper.

Advice to candidates
- Read each question carefully.
- Don't spend too long on one question.
- In calculations show clearly how you worked out your answers.
- If you have time at the end, go back and check your answers.

For examiner's use

Q	Attempt Nº			Q	Attempt Nº		
	1	2	3		1	2	3
1				5			
2				6			
3				7			
4							
Total							

Answer **all** questions in the spaces provided

Crude oil is made up of different fractions and these can be used as fuels. Burning different fractions releases different amounts of energy.

The amount of energy released when a fuel is burned can be measured by using it to heat water. The greater the temperature increase of the water, the more energy has been released by the fuel.

The fuel is placed in a spirit burner below a container of water. All of the fuel is burned and the maximum temperature reached by the water is measured.

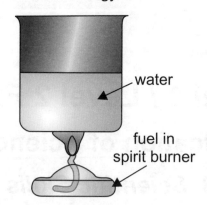

water

fuel in spirit burner

1   Lisbeth and Rico choose three different crude oil fractions. They want to find out which one of the fractions releases the most energy when burned.

They are going to burn the three fractions to find out which one causes the temperature of the water to increase the most.

(a)   Lisbeth writes a risk assessment for the investigation.

Explain **two** precautions that Lisbeth should take in this investigation.

1 ....

....

....

....

2 ....

....

....

....

(4 marks)

(b) What is the dependent variable in Lisbeth and Rico's investigation?

....

(1 mark)

(c) Rico says that the same mass of each fuel should be burned.

Give **two** other variables that should be controlled in the investigation.

1 ....

2 ....

(2 marks)

7

Turn over▶

52

2   In another investigation you could look at whether the amount of fat in a food affects the amount of energy it releases when it is burned.

Leave blank

(a)   One of the variables in this investigation is the amount of fat in a food.
What type of variable is this?

....

(1 mark)

(b)   Write a hypothesis for how the amount of fat in a food affects the amount of energy it releases when it is burned.

....

....

....

....

....

....

(2 marks)

(c) Write a plan for this investigation.

....

....

....

....

....

....

....

....

....

....

....

(6 marks)

$\frac{}{9}$

Turn over▶

3 Sofia carried out an investigation into the effect of increasing the surface area of a parachute on how long it takes to fall from a height.

Each parachute was made from a square of polythene. String was tied to each corner of the square and the strings were secured to a weight.

Sofia made parachutes with different surface areas and dropped them from a height. She measured how long it took the parachutes to reach the ground using a stopwatch. She repeated the test four times for each size of parachute.

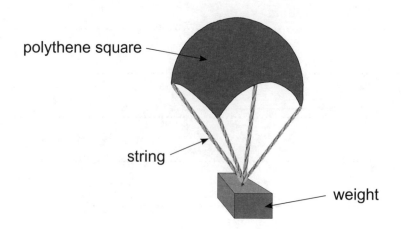

Sofia's results are shown below.

Parachute area (cm^2)	Time to fall (s)				Mean
	1	2	3	4	
25	4.2	4.6	4.3	4.4	
36	6.9	5.1	7.2	7.1	
49	9.7	9.6	9.5	9.3	

(a) One of Sofia's results is anomalous.

Give **two** possible errors Sofia could have made to produce this anomalous result.

1 ....

....

2 ....

....

(2 marks)

(b) Calculate the mean result for each parachute area, to two significant figures.

Write the means in the correct column in the table.

(2 marks)

(c) Explain how the data shows that increasing the air resistance on a parachute increases the time it takes to fall to the ground.

....

....

....

....

(2 marks)

(d) Sofia works out that the parachutes with a surface area of 49 cm² fall at an average speed of 8.2 m/s.

Use the equation below and the data from the table to calculate how far the parachutes fall, to two significant figures.

distance (m) = speed (m/s) × time (s)

distance .... m

(2 marks)

8

Turn over ▶

4 Endothermic reactions are chemical reactions that take in heat energy.

Gemma wanted to find an alternative to an 'ice pack'.

Her idea was a strong pack containing a bag of solid and water.

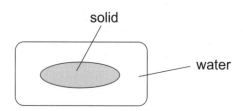

solid

water

When the bag of solid bursts, the solid will dissolve in water in an endothermic reaction.

Gemma carried out an investigation into some reactions she could use.

She mixed 5 g of powdered solid with 50 cm³ of water in a plastic cup and measured the temperature change.

Here are her results.

Chemical used	Temperature at start	Temperature at end
ammonium nitrate	22	7
anhydrous copper sulfate	22	31
potassium nitrate	22	15

(a) What important piece of information is missing from the table of results?

....

(1 mark)

(b) One of the reactions would be unsuitable.
State which reaction and explain why.

....

....

(1 mark)

(c) Explain which reaction would be the best to use for the 'ice pack'.

....

....

(1 mark)

58

(d)   One of Gemma's classmates was investigating different exothermic reactions for use in a 'heat pack'.

Five different chemical reactions were tested and the temperature rise recorded. The results are shown below.

Reaction	Temperature rise (°C)
1	10
2	21
3	53
4	17
5	26

Draw a bar chart of these results using the graph paper below.

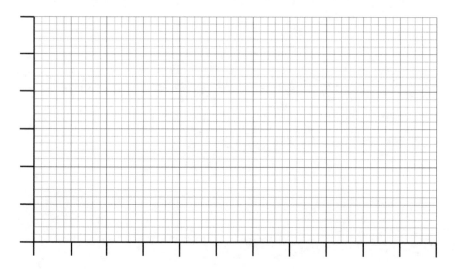

(4 marks)

7

5   Falak wanted to find out how the concentration of acid affects the amount of heat energy produced in a neutralisation reaction.

He measured out 25 cm³ of sodium hydroxide solution into a beaker and added 0.5 moles/dm³ hydrochloric acid (HCl) to the sodium hydroxide solution.

He measured the temperature of the sodium hydroxide before and after the acid was added, and recorded the temperature increase.

Falak repeated the experiment with different concentrations of hydrochloric acid. His results are shown on the line graph below.

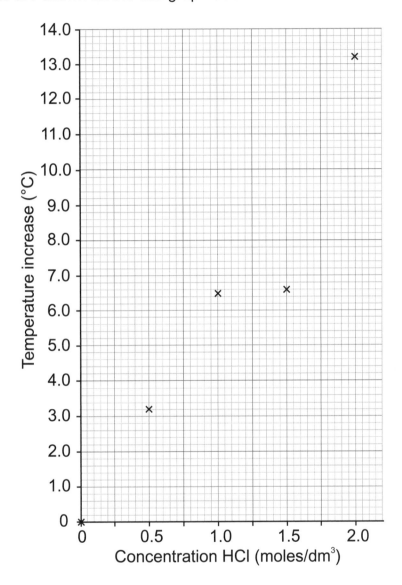

(a)   Draw a line of best fit to complete the graph.

(2 marks)

(b)   Use the graph to estimate what the temperature increase would be if Falak added 0.75 moles/dm³ HCl to the sodium hydroxide.

....

(1 mark)

Turn over▶

(c) Lois wants to repeat Falak's investigation but there is not enough detail in Falak's method.

Give **two** more pieces of information that Lois would need to repeat the investigation.

1 ....

....

2 ....

....

(2 marks)

5

6 Arlene repeats Falak's investigation but uses a lower concentration of sodium hydroxide.

Arlene's results are shown below.

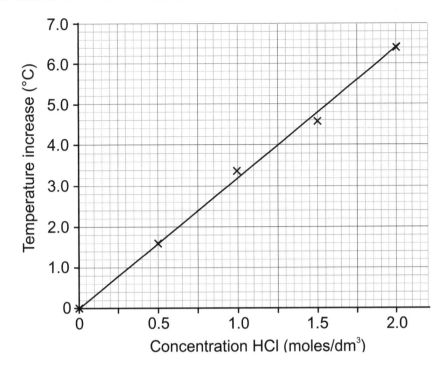

(a) Describe the trend in Arlene's results.

....

....

....

....

....

....

(3 marks)

Turn over▶

(b) Arlene decides to repeat her investigation.

Give **two** reasons why this is a good idea.

1 ....

....

2 ....

....

(2 marks)

5

7   Antibiotics can be used to kill bacteria and help a patient fight disease.

Adil carried out an investigation to test the following hypothesis:

Antibiotic X will be the most effective antibiotic at killing bacteria.

Adil did the following:

- he grew one type of bacteria on top of agar jelly in a Petri dish.

- he soaked paper discs in three different antibiotics (X, Y and Z) and water.

- he put the discs on top of the agar in the Petri dish.

- he kept the dish at 35 °C for two days

Adil's results are shown in the picture and table below.

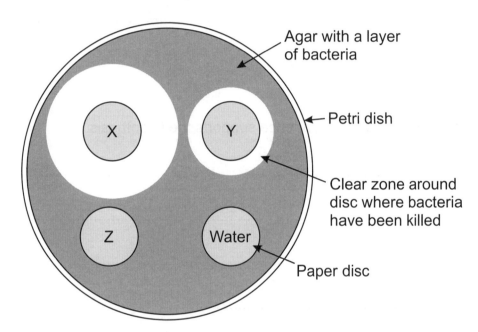

Disc	Clear zone (mm)
X	4
Y	2.5
Z	0
Water	0

Turn over▶

64

(a) (i) Write a suitable conclusion for this experiment.

....

....

(1 mark)

(ii) Explain how the results of the investigation support your conclusion.

....

....

....

....

(2 marks)

(b) Explain to what extent the evidence supports the hypothesis.

....

....

....

....

(2 marks)

(c) Explain **two** ways in which the experiment could be extended to provide further evidence for the hypothesis.

1 ....

....

....

2 ....

....

....

(4 marks)

END OF QUESTIONS

Answers

Section One — Planning

Pages 8-9

1) b) The number of bacteria increases.
2) Spilling acid on his skin.
3) a) hazards
   b) reduce
   c) plan
4) a) true
   b) true
   c) false — The steps in the method need to be in the order you'd carry them out.
5)

Reason: It's used to measure out volumes of liquid.

6) a) Increasing the amount of magnesium used will increase the amount of heat given off.
   b) To measure the temperature (of the reaction).
   c) 1 — Measure out 50 cm³ of hydrochloric acid into a measuring cylinder.
      2 — Pour the hydrochloric acid into a beaker.
      3 — Add the magnesium ribbon to the beaker and start the stopwatch.
      4 — Measure the temperature of the reaction after one minute.
   d) Hazard: She will be using acid.
      To reduce the risk: She will wear safety goggles and a lab coat.

Pages 12-13

1) a) The angle of the slope.
   b) The distance the marble travels.
   c) The size of the marble.
2) Four measurements, 1 mg - 15 mg
3) three
4) a) Three or more masses that are not too close together. For example, 2 g, 4 g, 6 g, 8 g, 10 g.
   b) By always using 25 cm³ of acid.
5) a) The concentration of acid.
   b) The temperature of the reaction.
   c) For example, temperature of the sodium hydroxide. / Volume of acid. / Volume of sodium hydroxide. / Concentration of sodium hydroxide.

Section Two — Presenting and Analysing Data

Pages 20-23

1)

Wire	Repeat 1 (Ω)	Repeat 2 (Ω)	Repeat 3 (Ω)
1	5	4	5
2	9	10	8

2) a) A result that doesn't fit in with the other results.
   b) 43
   c) 49.5
3) $\dfrac{13 + 10 + 12}{3}$
4) Antibiotic A:
   $(7 + 6 + 8) \div 3 = 7$ mm
   Antibiotic B:
   $(1 + 3 + 2) \div 3 = 2$ mm
5) 10 °C:
   $(52 + 53 + 52) \div 3 = 52.3$ s
   20 °C:
   $(40 + 40 + 41) \div 3 = 40.3$ s
   30 °C:
   $(29 + 28 + 31) \div 3 = 29.3$ s
6) $mass = \dfrac{force}{acceleration}$
7) a)

	Force (N)	Distance (m)	Work done (J)
Block 1	5.2	0.25	1.3
Block 2	12.6	0.5	6.3

   b) There are 100 cm in 1 m.
      This means 1200 cm ÷ 100 = 12 m
8) a) $10 - 6 = 4$ g
   b) $percentage\ change = \dfrac{difference}{starting\ amount} \times 100$

   $percentage\ change = \dfrac{4}{6} \times 100$

   $percentage\ change = 66.7\%$
9) a) 33.5
   b) The reaction wasn't at the correct temperature.
   c) $(43.0 + 41.5 + 42.5) \div 3 = 42.3$ s
   d) 33.5 is an anomalous result so is left out of the equation.
      $(22.0 + 21.5) \div 2 = 21.8$ s
   e) 70 °C

Pages 28-31

1)

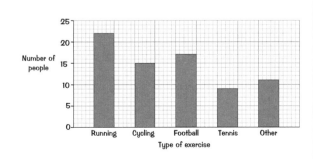

2)

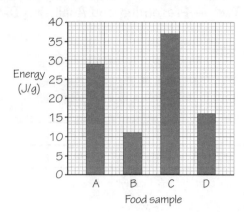

3)

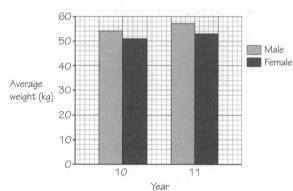

4)

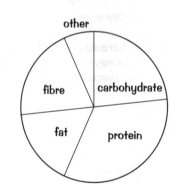

5) a) $10 + 4 + 9 + 4 + 3 = 30$ people

   b) $\dfrac{360}{30} = 12$

   c) $10 \times 12 = 120°$

6) a) and b)

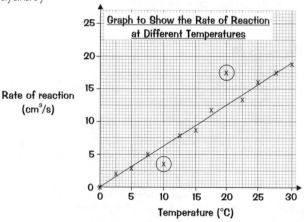

7) a), b) and c)

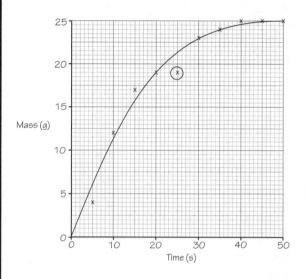

Pages 36-39

1) a) 12 seconds
   b) 4 m/s
   c) 21 m/s
2) a) $31 - 21 = 10\,°C$
   b) $30 - 27 = 3\,°C$
3) a) 120 beats per minute
   b) 70 beats per minute
   c) 170 beats per minute
   d) 13 seconds
4) a) A — change in y
       B — change in x
   b) $40 - 20 = 20$
   c) $4 - 2 = 2$
   d) $\dfrac{80}{2} = 40$
5) a) 20 seconds
   b) 37 metres
   c) Distance Sarah had walked after 25 seconds = 37 metres
       Distance Sarah had walked after 40 seconds = 60 metres
       Difference = 60 – 37 = 23 metres
   d) For example, draw a triangle like this:

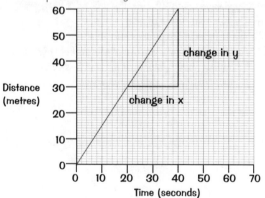

Change in y = 60 – 30 = 30 metres
Change in x = 40 – 20 = 20 seconds
Gradient = $\dfrac{\text{change in y}}{\text{change in x}} = \dfrac{30}{20} = 1.5$

Answers

Pages 42-43

1) a) Positive correlation
   b) Directly proportional
2) As time doubles, the mass of product made doubles.
3) a) Positive correlation.
   b) As the concentration of hydrochloric acid increases, the temperature increases.
   c) As the concentration of hydrochloric acid doubles, the temperature also doubles.
   d) Directly proportional

Section Three — Conclusion and Evaluation

Pages 46-47

1) Food sample A produces more heat energy than samples B or C when burnt.
2) a) As temperature increases, the rate of reaction also increases.
   b) yes
3) a) As voltage across the thermistor increases, the current through it increases.
   b) No. The current through the thermistor increases as the voltage across it increases.
   c) For example, there may have been a problem with the equipment used to measure the voltage or current.

Practice Exam

Pages 49-64

1) (a) For example: she should keep flammable items away from the spirit burner [1 mark] to reduce the risk of fire [1 mark]. She should not touch the equipment without protective gloves [1 mark] to reduce the risk of burns from hot equipment [1 mark].
   (b) The temperature of the water [1 mark].
   (c) Any two from: for example, the volume of water / the type of water container / the type of spirit burner [1 mark each].
2) (a) independent [1 mark]
   (b) For example: the more fat a food contains, the more energy it will release when it is burned [1 mark]. If you double the amount of fat in a food, the energy released when it is burned will double [1 mark].
   (c) How to grade your answer:
   O marks: No relevant points are made.
   1-2 marks: A brief description of how to carry out the investigation is given, including some equipment, one control variable and some measurements.
   3-4 marks: Some description of how to carry out the investigation is given, including the most suitable equipment, two control variables and the range of measurements. The steps are written in the order you'd carry them out in.

5-6 marks: A detailed description of how to carry out the investigation is given, including the most suitable equipment, more than two control variables and the range of measurements. The steps are written in the order you'd carry them out in and how the method will test the hypothesis is explained.

Here are some points your answer may include:
Weigh a small sample of food using scales.
Put the food sample on a (mounted) needle.
Measure out 50 ml of water into a copper calorimeter using a measuring cylinder.
Take the temperature of the water using a thermometer.
Light the food sample and put it under the calorimeter.
Let the food burn out.
Make a note of the highest temperature the water reaches.
Reweigh any of the food sample left.
Repeat with different types of food with different amounts of fat (for example, peanuts, marshmallows).
Use the same scales, the same volume of water, the same thermometer and the same calorimeter each time.
Calculate the amount of energy released by each food sample and compare it to the amount of fat in each food.

3) (a) Any two from: for example, she may have mis-read the stopwatch / the parachute may have been dropped from the wrong height / the parachute may not have opened properly [1 mark each].
   (b)

Parachute area (cm^2)	Time to fall (s)				Mean
	1	2	3	4	
25	4.2	4.6	4.3	4.4	4.4
36	6.9	5.1	7.2	7.1	7.1
49	9.7	9.6	9.5	9.3	9.5

[2 marks for all three means correct to two significant figures, ignoring anomalous result (5.1 s). Otherwise 1 mark for three means correct including the anomalous result.]
   (c) Increasing the surface area of the parachute increases the air resistance [1 mark]. When the surface area of the parachute (and therefore the air resistance) is bigger, it takes longer to fall to the ground [1 mark].
   (d) distance (m) = speed (m/s) × time (s)
   distance = 8.2 m/s × 9.5 s = 78 m
   [2 marks for correct answer to two significant figures. Otherwise 1 mark for correct calculation using the mean value for time worked out for part (b)]

Answers

4) (a)   the unit of temperature *[1 mark]*
   (b)   The anhydrous copper sulfate reaction because it gives a temperature increase/is exothermic *[1 mark]*.
   (c)   The ammonium nitrate reaction as it produces the greatest decrease in temperature *[1 mark]*.
   (d)

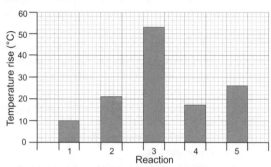

[1 mark for labelling axes to match table, 1 mark for appropriate scale on y axis, plus 1 mark for three bars drawn correctly or 2 marks for five bars drawn correctly]

5) (a)

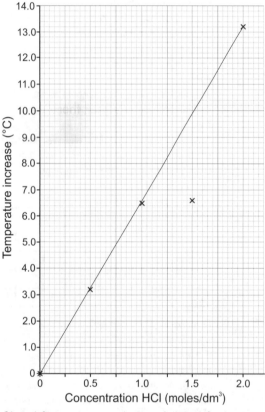

[1 mark for ignoring anomalous result, 1 mark for drawing a <u>straight</u> line of best fit]
   (b)   5.0 °C (accept 4.5-5.5 °C) *[1 mark]*
   (c)   The concentration of the sodium hydroxide solution *[1 mark]* and the volume of the hydrochloric acid *[1 mark]*.

6) (a)   As the concentration of hydrochloric acid goes up, the temperature increase does too *[1 mark]*. There is a directly proportional relationship between the concentration of hydrochloric acid and the temperature increase *[1 mark]*. When the concentration doubles, the temperature increase doubles *[1 mark]*.
   (b)   Repeating the experiment will help to identify anomalous results *[1 mark]*. It will also allow Arlene to calculate mean values for the results *[1 mark]*.

7) (a) (i)   Antibiotic X is more effective at killing this type of bacteria than antibiotics Y and Z *[1 mark]*.
       (ii)   Antibiotic X caused a bigger clear zone around the disc of 4 mm than antibiotic Y at 2.5 mm *[1 mark]* and antibiotic Z at 0 mm *[1 mark]*.
   (b)   The evidence partly supports the hypothesis because it shows that antibiotic X is more effective than the other antibiotics tested (Y and Z) at killing this type of bacteria *[1 mark]*. But it doesn't show that antibiotic X is more effective at killing all types of bacteria than all other antibiotics *[1 mark]*.
   (c)   For example: the experiment could be repeated using a wider range of antibiotics *[1 mark]*. This would show whether antibiotic X is still the most effective at killing bacteria *[1 mark]*. The experiment could be repeated using different types of bacteria *[1 mark]*. This would show whether antibiotic X is still the most effective at killing all types of bacteria *[1 mark]*.

Glossary

Anomalous result	A result that doesn't fit in with the rest of the results.
Bar chart	A type of graph where bars are used to show the size of each category of results.
Conclusion	A summary of what you've found after analysing your data.
Control variables	The things that are kept the same in an experiment.
Correlation	A relationship (link) between two things.
Curve of best fit	A curve on a graph which passes through or as near to as many of the points as possible.
Dependent variable	The thing that's measured in an experiment.
Directly proportional	A relationship between two things where they both increase (or decrease) by the same amount.
Evaluation	Where you say how well your investigation went and whether there were any problems.
Gradient	The slope of a graph.
Hazard	Something that causes a risk.
Hypothesis	A statement that says how two or more things could be linked. It is tested in an investigation.
Independent variable	The thing you change in an experiment.
Indirectly proportional	A relationship between two things where one increases and the other decreases by the same amount.
Line graph	A graph where a straight line or a curve shows the pattern of the plotted points.
Line of best fit	A line on a graph which passes through or as near to as many of the points as possible.
Mean	The average of a set of results.
Method	A step-by-step list of everything you would do in an experiment.
Negative correlation	A relationship where as one thing increases, the other thing decreases.

Glossary and Index

Pie chart	A round chart that is divided into sectors. Each sector shows the size of a category of results.
Plan	A description of what you're going to do in an investigation and how you're going to do it.
Positive correlation	A relationship where as one thing increases, so does the other.
Quantitative relationship	A relationship between two things where they both change by a certain amount.
Range of data	How far apart the highest and lowest measurements are.
Risk assessment	Spotting the hazards in an experiment and coming up with ways to reduce the risks from the hazards.

Index